WILD ANIMALS

The regal lion, the wily buffalo, the irascible rhino, the mighty elephant and the elusive leopard – these are the 'Big Five' of the African savannas, widely feared for the danger they present to humans and highly prized as trophy animals. It was not, in fact, their size alone that earned the 'Big Five' their place at the top of the list of wild creatures that demand respect, but also the risks involved in hunting them: all five of these animals are extremely dangerous when injured or cornered.

The dubious honour for the most feared animal is often shared by the lion and the buffalo. A full-grown lion *(above)*, though it may look sleepy, has long been respected for the life-threatening danger it represents. An angry, growling lion, dropped into a crouch, its ears back and its tail tip flicking rapidly from side to side, will give pause to the boldest of adventurers.

A wounded buffalo *(opposite, left)* has a reputation for savagery and cunning, and not without reason, as it has been known to circle and ambush a hunter following its spoor. A herd of buffalo may appear placid to the onlooker but these belligerent bovines will not hesitate to use their massive horns to ram and gore if they perceive any threat whatsoever.

The notoriously temperamental rhino *(opposite, below right)* has keen senses of smell and hearing but very poor eyesight. Although it may appear heavy and ungainly, a rhino can put on a surprising and agile turn of speed when threatened.

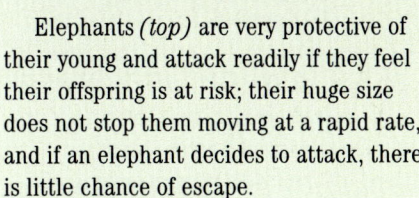

Elephants *(top)* are very protective of their young and attack readily if they feel their offspring is at risk; their huge size does not stop them moving at a rapid rate, and if an elephant decides to attack, there is little chance of escape.

The powerful leopard *(above right)* is by nature a shy and retiring creature but when trapped, wounded or threatened it can be extremely dangerous.

Although most animals will attack only if taken by surprise, and often prefer flight to fight, it is unwise to generalise and all animals should be treated with respect.

The 'Big Five', once widely distributed throughout Africa, are now restricted to areas mainly set aside for their protection.

All members of the cat family, Felidae, are highly specialised hunters. They are adept stalkers and killers, and have curved claws (which are retractable in all species except the cheetah) and sharp teeth that are adapted to slicing food into chunks small enough to swallow.

The most sociable members of the cat family are lions *(above)*, which live in prides that may number up to thirty individuals led by a dominant male. Although the females do most of the hunting, the adult males always eat first, followed by the females. The cubs are left to fight over the remainders of the kill.

Serval *(left)* are recognisable by the distinctive coloration of the backs of their ears, which have a black band separated from the black ear tip by a white patch. These agile cats, befitting their relatively small size, hunt mainly small mammals but do sometimes take the young of smaller antelope species.

Cheetahs *(opposite, above)* have the reputation of being the fastest animals on earth, and use their ability for high-speed chases over short distances to bring down prey. These diurnal hunters are often chased off their kills by more aggressive lions or hyenas.

The African wild cat *(opposite, below left)* closely resembles a domestic cat but is larger, with longer legs, and may further be differentiated by the rich, reddish-brown coloration of the backs of its ears.

The leopard *(opposite, below right)* is mainly solitary and nocturnal, and hunts its prey using a combination of stealth and strength. It is able to drag heavy prey up a tree, out of reach of hyenas and lions.

The aardwolf *(top)*, belying its dog-like appearance and well-developed canines, is not a meat-eater but a specialised feeder on termites. It moves about at night, locating its nocturnal ant prey using its senses of smell and hearing, and then licks up the termites using its long, sticky, mobile tongue. An aardwolf will dig its own burrow, but will also readily use burrows excavated and then abandoned by other species. This animal has suffered for its wolf-like appearance, having been persecuted for stock destruction that is most often attributable to jackals.

Blackbacked jackals *(above)*, active hunters of small prey, do not hesitate to take young livestock, and are therefore considered 'problem animals' in some farming areas. Wily creatures, they appear able to evade all but the most cunningly devised traps.

The Cape fox *(opposite, left)* is an inoffensive little animal which lies up in holes in the ground during the day and emerges at night to feed on insects, mice and other small mammals, the occasional reptile, and birds and their eggs.

African wild dogs *(above)*, one of the most endangered large carnivores on the continent, are known for both their ruthless pack-hunting skills and their highly organised social behaviour. Only one pair in a pack, the alpha male and female, mates and reproduces, while the other members help with the rearing and feeding of the young pups.

The spotted hyena *(right)*, once thought to be a cowardly scavenger, is now known to be an efficient hunter. It does, however, readily eat carrion, and it is not unknown for a pack of hyenas to drive lions or other predators from their kills.

African elephants, at masses of up to 5 500 kilograms the largest living land mammals, are creatures of the savanna woodland but can be surprisingly adaptable, as has been borne out by the 'desert elephants' of the arid Kaokoland in northern Namibia and the forest-dwelling elephants of Central and West Africa. All elephants need water both for drinking – an adult consumes about 160 litres a day – and for thermo-regulation. During hot, dry periods, they use their huge ears as cooling aids: the backs of the ears are well supplied with blood vessels and when flapped act as convectors, cooling the blood. Elephants' ears are also an accurate indication as to their mood – to which anyone who has witnessed an angry elephant, mock-charging with its ears held outwards, can attest.

Elephants have prodigious appetites, daily eating anything up to 200 kilograms of browse, or green grass during the rainy season. Although not specialist feeders, individuals do develop tastes for certain plant species and may travel vast distances in search of their particular food preference. Strict herbivores, elephants eat tree bark and roots, leaves, softer branches and fruit such as that of the baobab and acacia pods. They can be destructive feeders and, if left unchecked, sometimes destroy entire habitats, endangering both themselves and those that share their environment.

The trunk is very versatile, and elephants are able to use it to manipulate even very tiny objects. It is used for pulling

browse from trees, for sucking up water to spray into the mouth or behind the ears, for touching, dusting, smelling, lifting and sound production – truly an indispensable tool for any elephant!

The tusks, which in particularly large species have been known to weigh up to 100 kilograms, are actually incisor teeth and are used for digging, breaking branches and in fighting. Some individuals do not have tusks or have tusks which are reduced in size. This is thought to be a genetic throw-back because populations with large tusks were killed off by poachers. Small, brittle tusks, like those of Etosha's elephants, are due to a mineral deficiency.

Elephants are long-lived and may survive for up to 70 years. Their lifespan is determined by their dentition: they have six pairs of molars, with two in use at a time, these being replaced by the next pair when they have been worn down. Once all six pairs of molars have been worn down, the elephant is unable to chew and dies through lack of nutrition.

The social organisation of elephants takes the form of a matriarchy, with a dominant female leading a family group. Males, which may be solitary or move in small groups, join the family herds only when the cows are in oestrus. Females have their first calf at around 11 years of age.

Once widely distributed over much of Africa, the rhino has been brought to the verge of extinction by intensive poaching to feed the insatiable demand for rhino horn in the Far East. Aside from man, an adult rhino has few natural enemies, although the young are sometimes taken by particularly bold lions.

The two main rhino species that occur in Africa appear similar at first glance but are actually quite easy to tell apart. The hook-lipped or black rhino *(left)* has a prehensile upper lip which is necessary for its browsing habits, while the much larger square-lipped or white rhino *(above)* is a grazer and therefore has a squared-off, broad mouth.

White rhinos tend to be more sociable than their bad-tempered cousins, and may form family groups; black rhinos, on the other hand, tend to be solitary and are rarely seen as they prefer thick, bushy habitat. A reliable source of drinking water is an essential for both rhino species, which also enjoy mud-wallowing, both to keep cool and to control ectoparasites such as ticks, which become trapped in the mud and then fall off when the mud dries and hardens.

The stately giraffe can grow to a height of five metres and, in spite of the amazing length of its neck, has only seven vertebrae – the same number as man. Giraffes can move at speed, their lumbering gallop carrying them swiftly along in a rocking horse motion while the tail moves in a circular direction.

Giraffes appear to be able to subsist on the moisture gleaned from their browse and so do not require regular access to water; when they do drink, they generally do so in a state of high tension, as the awkward, splayed-legged posture they need to adopt in order to

reach the water's surface renders them vulnerable to attack by lion. When a giraffe lowers its head to drink, special valves in the arteries prevent the blood from rushing into the brain.

Giraffes have long, prehensile tongues especially adapted for pulling twigs and leaves from between the thorns of their favourite foodplant, acacia trees.

Social structure is loose, with females and young gathering in groups that frequently change composition. Mating can take place at any time of year, and bulls move from herd to herd, mating with females in oestrus. Occasionally males will spar over the right to mate with a female, using their long necks to swing their heads at each other like clubs, but serious damage is seldom done. Giraffes give birth to one calf after a gestation period of about 15 months. Although the calf can stand and walk shortly after birth, the mother keeps her calf isolated from the rest of the herd for about three weeks after the birth, returning frequently to suckle and clean it.

Although they are docile creatures, giraffes do not hesitate to defend themselves, using their front hooves to devastating effect.

The surly-looking, ox-like buffalo *(opposite and below left)* are gregarious creatures, living in herds that may number in the thousands. Buffalo are quick-tempered and can be very dangerous and cunning adversaries. Their habitat requirements include plenty of shade, water and grass, and mud-wallows for keeping cool and controlling ectoparasites. They tend to drink in the cooler hours of the early morning and late afternoon, resting up during the heat of the day and often grazing at night.

Three species of zebra occur in Africa, the most common and widespread of which is Burchell's zebra *(above and right)*. This species can be identified by the 'shadow stripes' between the black stripes on the hindquarters. The Cape mountain zebra *(below right)* is relatively rare and has a restricted range; it can be told from its cousin in that it lacks the 'shadow stripes', and by the 'grid-iron' pattern on its rump.

Zebra are preyed upon by many carnivores, lion chief among them. The zebra's bold stripes may appear to stand out against the dun hues of the bush, but serve the purpose of confusing predators, which find it difficult to single out an individual in a herd. Zebra are quick to defend themselves, however, and will kick and bite vigorously.

A large and majestic antelope, the kudu *(left)* is well known for its remarkable jumping ability, and is able to leap with ease, from a standstill, to a height of two metres. A feature of the males is the beautiful, symmetrical, spiralling horns, which are used in combat over mating rights to oestrous females; males fighting during the rut have been known to inextricably lock horns and later die of starvation. Males form bachelor herds or move about on their own, joining up with females only during the mating season. Although kudu are mainly browsers, they have become a pest in some farming areas as they have a predilection for crops such as lucerne, maize and vegetables.

Male nyala *(above)* resemble male kudu, but have less spiralled horns and a heavy fringe of hair hanging below the belly; like kudu, they form bachelor groups or live solitarily, joining up with female herds during the rut. Female nyala are hornless, much smaller than the males and have an orange coat clearly marked with vertical white stripes.

Driven by their need for water and their partiality for fresh, sprouting grass, blue wildebeest *(above)* have long been known for their spectacular migrations during which several thousand animals undertake long journeys to new feeding grounds. Sadly, their numbers have been depleted in recent times and wildebeest migrations on this scale are now rarely seen except in the Serengeti-Masai Mara ecosystem. The mating season tends to take place during autumn, with most of the calves being dropped in summer.

The startlingly handsome sable *(right)* with their magnificent, swept-back horns live in herds of up to thirty individuals. During the breeding season, males establish territories which they defend vigorously; some territorial clashes lead to the death of the combatants.

The klipspringer *(left)* is easily identified as it is the only antelope that walks on the tips of its hooves on rounded boulders. The hooves are rubbery in order to afford these little antelope purchase in their rocky habitat. The coat of the klipspringer is made up of springy, spiny hair which protects it from hard knocks and keeps it warm and dry.

The common duiker *(above)* takes its name from its habit of diving into cover when threatened. Although generally quiet and secretive, it will fight furiously if cornered or surprised.

Impalas *(opposite, below)* are one of the most common of Africa's small antelope. Their quiet lives change during the rut, when large breeding herds form, overseen by a dominant male. Males competing for access to oestrous females may aggressively disrupt breeding herds, giving roars and grunts, and do battle with the resident male for possession of the herd.

The inquisitive oribi *(below left)* is an attractive, medium-sized antelope found in small groups in open, hilly grasslands. They commonly lie up in tall grass with the head erect, keeping a watchful eye out for danger. When alarmed, they bound off with a distinctive stotting action, leaping straight-legged into the air.

The blesbok *(right)* aggregates in very large herds during the dry winter months. Blesbok have the unusual characteristic of standing in groups with their heads down and oriented towards the sun.

Eland *(below right)*, Africa's largest antelope, are often depicted in Bushman paintings. An important food source, these bulky antelope were held in high esteem by the hunter-gatherers who vanished from their mountain refuges in the Drakensberg and other regions of southern Africa more than a century ago. Despite its size, the agile eland can clear a two-metre fence with ease.

Male hippo *(above)* establish pear-shaped territories in water, and aggressively defend these against other males, often seriously injuring each other. Semi-aquatic, hippo spend much of their day lolling in water or on sand banks; they secrete an oily substance that protects their surprisingly delicate skin from sun damage. At night they leave the water to feed, often covering considerable distances. They have large appetites, and are highly selective grazers on grass and young reed shoots.

The playful Cape clawless otter *(left)* is largely aquatic, although it does spend a considerable amount of time out of the water, often passing the hours sunbathing in a variety of postures. The fingers are very dexterous, and these otters find much of their food by feeling about in mud.

Waterbuck *(above)* are seldom found far from water. They are largely left alone by predators, as they secrete a musky-smelling, waterproofing substance which gives their flesh an unpleasant taste.

The hinged terrapin *(left)* is commonly seen in large water bodies, basking on logs and rocks during the day. These terrapins scavenge at game killed by crocodiles, and take ticks from the legs of drinking buffalo and other large animals.

The Nile crocodile *(left)* hatches about three months after the eggs are laid. Female crocodiles exhibit a high degree of maternal involvement, keeping watch near the nest site during incubation, and responding to the cheeps of the hatching crocodiles by digging open the nest site and carrying the hatchlings to water before washing and releasing them.

G emsbok *(left)*, or oryx, have several interesting adaptations to enable them to survive in their harsh, arid environment. One of these is the ability to control their core temperature by a system of blood vessels in the nose which cools the blood circulating to the brain. Gemsbok obtain moisture from their food, eating melons and digging roots and bulbs out of the ground.

Springbok *(below)*, similarly, inhabit the drier parts of southern Africa, including the Kalahari, and, when water is scarce, are able to obtain moisture from their food.

The little bateared fox *(opposite, above left)* uses its enormous ears to locate its subterranean prey, wandering about and periodically turning its head to the ground to listen for movement, before digging termites and other morsels out of the substrate.

Suricates *(right)* are highly sociable animals, living together in warrens and surviving on a diet of snakes, desert insects and other invertebrates.

The ground squirrel *(below)*, which sometimes shares living space with a family of suricates, makes good use of its large, bushy tail as a sun shade while it forages for food.

The endearingly ugly warthog *(above left)* is a burrow dweller, depending on this retreat to protect it from adverse climatic conditions and hungry predators. Warthogs are capable of digging their own burrows but they sometimes take over the abandoned retreats of other animals, such as ant-bears.

The dwarf mongoose *(above right)* is a playful, gregarious animal, living in groups of ten or more and engaging in much mutual grooming. Dwarf mongooses often make their home in burrows in termitaria, but can also dig their own.

Baboons *(left)* are sociable creatures, and grooming is an important part of their daily contact. They have a catholic diet, digging for roots and bulbs, eating insects and other invertebrates, and sometimes taking young antelope, mice and birds.

approached too closely. Although it is mainly nocturnal, it also moves about in the early morning and late afternoon.

The large-spotted genet *(below)* is sometimes mistaken for a civet but is much smaller. It is an inveterate tree climber, although it does much of its foraging on the ground. It eats a wide variety of invertebrates, but especially insects, and also takes small rodents, reptiles, amphibians, mammals and birds; occasionally it breaks into poultry runs in search of food. Like the pangolin, the large-spotted genet secretes an evil-smelling musk from its anal glands when under stress.

The pangolin *(top)* is a nocturnal anteater, and uses its curved, sharp front claws to open termite nests before inserting its long, glutinous tongue into the burrows to extract its food. Its heavy, imbricated scales are used in defence: when under threat, the pangolin curls up into a ball and anyone foolish enough to try to uncurl it may find his fingers lacerated by a sideways swipe of the sharp-scaled tail.

The civet *(above)* relies on its striped and blotched coat as camouflage, but will burst out of cover and run to safety if

The lesser bushbaby *(above left)* rests up during the day in trees in self-constructed nests of leaves, sticks and grass or in abandoned birds' nests. Strictly nocturnal, if disturbed during the day it will be very loath to wake up. It feeds on the gum of trees, particularly acacias, although it does also descend to the ground to forage for insects. It is completely at home among the branches, leaping or climbing around with great agility.

The locally common and widely distributed vervet monkey *(above)* makes its home in the heavy foliage of tall trees or in crevices in rocky areas. Diurnal, vervet monkeys move about in troops of up to twenty individuals, foraging for fruit, flowers, seed pods and leaves, insects, birds' eggs and young birds.

The tree squirrel *(left)* is very agile in its arboreal habitat, and is able to leap from tree to tree to reach the safety of its nesting hole if it perceives danger. Tree squirrels nest in holes in trees, usually those made by woodpeckers. They forage on the ground, taking flowers, leaves, bark, fruit and insects.